MW01629882

For YOU and ME!

Fall is...
Rhyme in Time Series

barbarapinke.com

First edition 2024

ISBN 978-3-949736-76-6 (paperback)
ISBN 978-3-949736-77-3 (hardcover)
ISBN 978-3-949736-78-0 (e-book)

Written by Barbara Pinke
Edited by Andrea Ketchelmeier
Illustrated by Alvin Adhi
Designed by Gábor Dinya

Publisher's Cataloging-in-Publication data

Names: Pinke, Barbara, author. | Adhi, Alvin, illustrator.
Title: Fall is... / written by Barbara Pinke; illustrated by Alvin Adhi.
Series: Rhyme in Time
Description: Barbara Pinke, 2024. | Summary: This book celebrates the magic of fall, highlighting crisp days, swirling leaves, pumpkin patches, and cozy treats. This short rhyming story takes readers on a heartwarming journey through the season's vibrant beauty and playful wonders.
Identifiers: ISBN: 978-3-949736-77-3 (hardcover) | 978-3-949736-76-6 (paperback) | 978-3-949736-78-0 (ebook)
Subjects: LCSH Autumn--Juvenile fiction. | Seasons--Juvenile fiction. | Stories in verse.
| BISAC JUVENILE FICTION / Concepts / Seasons
Classification: LCC PZ7.1 .P56 Fa 2024 | DDC [E]--dc23

Written by
Barbara Pinke

Illustrated by
Alvin Adhi

I have a poster on my wall
of winter, summer, spring, and fall.

Cold or warm or leafless tree,
every season's great to me.

Fall is cider in the cup.

Fall is squirrels stocking up.

Fall is brown and sometimes red.

Fall is slicing pumpkin bread.

Fall is going back to class.

Fall is handprints on the glass.

Fall is mushrooms everywhere.

Fall is wood smoke in the air.

Fall is lovely chilly nights.

Fall is dancing Northern Lights.

Fall is time for tricks and treats.

Fall is markets in the streets.

Fall is sweaters, light and warm.

Fall is wind that rides the storm.

Fall is grandpa's story time.
My superstar cat!
He's just like that.
He's silly

Fall is rocks and trees to climb.

Fall is birds up in the sky.

Fall is waving them goodbye.

Fall is boots on muddy trails.

Fall is sharing spooky tales.

Fall is here, and fall is there.

Fall is
magic everywhere.

ABOUT THE ILLUSTRATOR

Alvin Adhi is an illustrator who loves nature.
He loves to draw living things with any emotion that is contained in them.

Alvin is also an observer. Every shape, texture, and color fascinates him.
Falling leaves, children giggling happily in their Halloween costumes, and the activities
of animals welcoming the cooler season are his favorite things during the fall.

Besides drawing, he likes gardening and fishkeeping.
He hopes that through his art, he can put a smile on your face.

Email: alvintheillustrator@gmail.com
Facebook: @alvinadhi
Instagram: @alvin_adhi

ABOUT THE AUTHOR

Barbara Pinke is a multi-award-winning author who loves to create
stories and spice them up with adventure and fun.

She was born and raised in Hungary
and later hopscotched across Europe before settling in Germany.

Website: barbarapinke.com
Email: barbara@barbarapinke.com
Facebook and Instagram: @barbarapinke.author

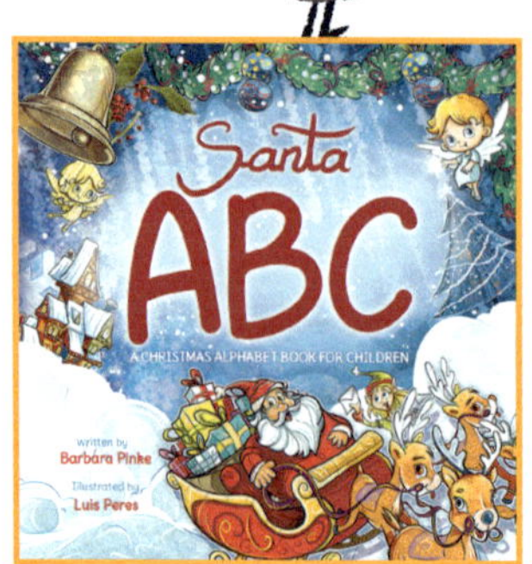

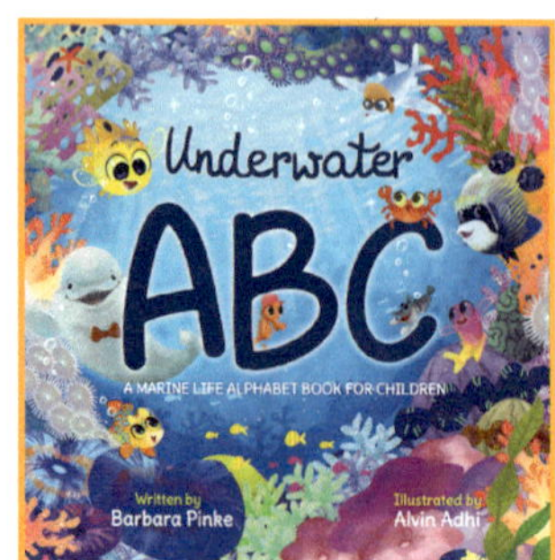

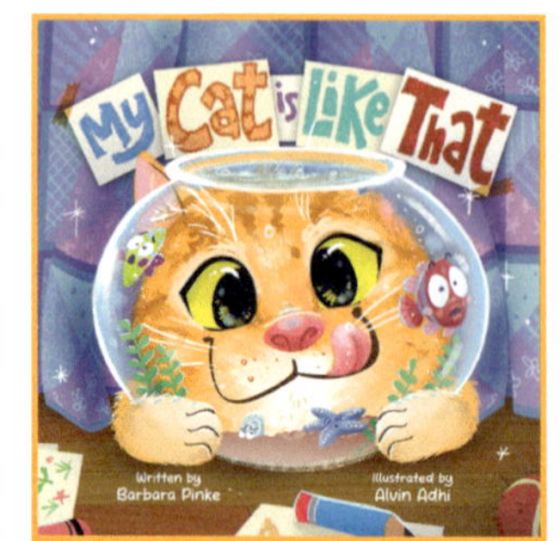

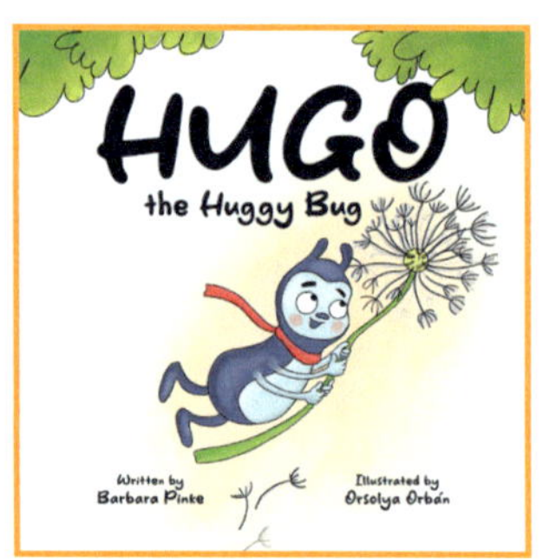

OTHER BOOKS
BY THE AUTHOR

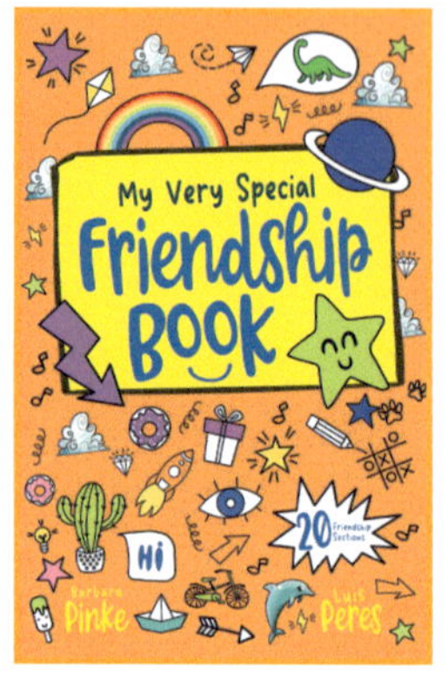

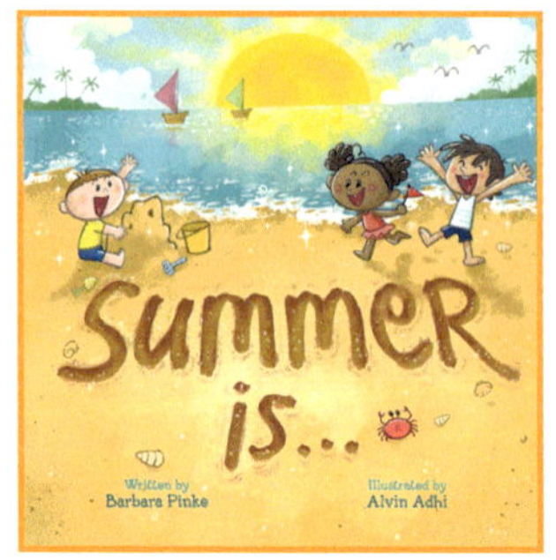

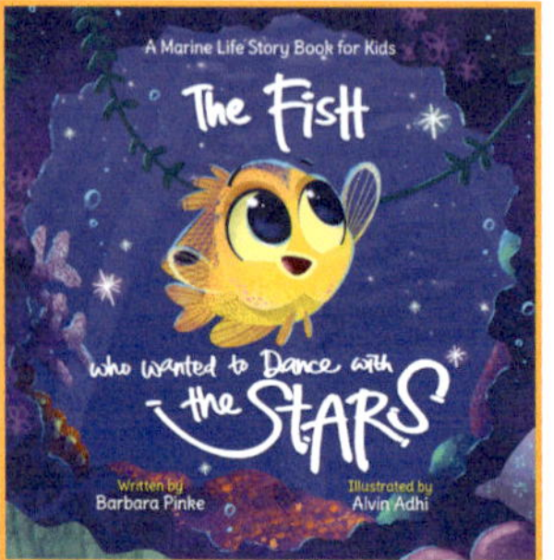

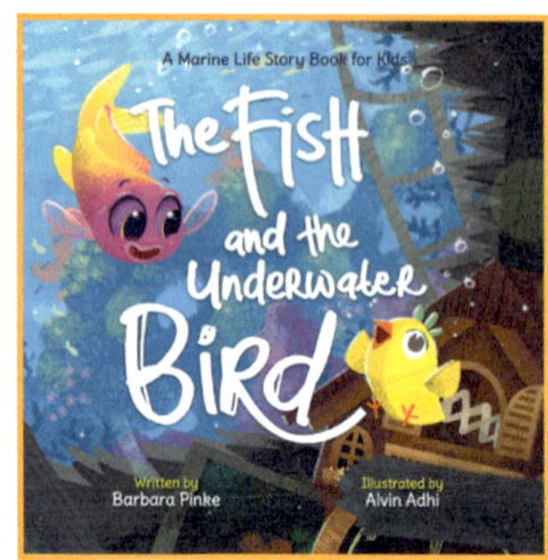

GET IN TOUCH

Scan this QR code to go to barbarapinke.com where you can find information about other adventures and a dedicated space, FunZone. Get your freebies: mazes, word searches, coloring sheets, and more.

I hope you have enjoyed my story. Your feedback is very important to me, and I would love to hear your thoughts on my work.
If you have a few moments, please consider leaving a review online.
Your review will not only help me improve my content,
but also help others who are looking for similar information.

Thank you in advance for your time and support!

 barbarapinke.com

 barbara@barbarapinke.com

 @barbarapinke.author

 @barbarapinkeauthor

You can also follow me on BookBub and Goodreads.

Made in United States
Cleveland, OH
09 November 2024